12 MILITARY LEADERS WHO CHANGED THE WORLD

by Matthew McCabe

12
STORY LIBRARY
MORE TO EXPLORE

www.12StoryLibrary.com

12-Story Library is an imprint of Bookstaves.

Photographs ©: Samuel H. Kress Collection/PD, cover, 1; Musée CROZATIER du Puy-en-Velay/PD, 4; Ángel M. Felicísimo/CC2.0, 5; Master Sgt. Kap Kim/US Army, 6; Sgt. Stephen Decatur/US Army, 7; Library of Congress, 8; Library of Congress, 9; John Opie/William Sharp/PD, 10; Paul Walter/CC2.0, 11; Everett Historical/Shutterstock.com, 12; Jacques Renier/CC2.5, 13; Expert Infantry/CC2.0, 14; Lynn Gilbert/CC4.0, 15; Samuel H. Kress Collection/PD, 16; Nagel Auktionen/PD, 17; Gordon Napier/CC2.5, 18; Betty Johnson/Alamy, 19; PD, 20; Musée du Louvre/PD, 21; National Maritime Museum/PD, 22; National Maritime Museum/PD, 23; US Navy, 24; 1st Class Kristopher Wilson/US Navy, 25; charistoone-images/Alamy, 26; vlasta2/CC2.0, 27; PD, 28; istanbulphotos/Shutterstock.com, 29

ISBN
9781632357175 (hardcover)
9781632358264 (paperback)
9781645820055 (ebook)

Library of Congress Control Number: 2019938647

Printed in the United States of America
July 2019

About the Cover

A portrait of Napoleon Bonaparte in 1812 by Jacques-Louis David.

Access free, up-to-date content on this topic plus a full digital version of this book. Scan the QR code on page 31 or use your school's login at 12StoryLibrary.com.

Table of Contents

Julius Caesar: The Man Who Made an Empire 4

Khatol Mohammadzai: Jumping into the History Books 6

Ulysses S. Grant: The Man Who Saved the Union 8

Queen Boudica: From Teen to Warrior Queen 10

Charles Martel: The Man They Called "The Hammer" 12

Rear Admiral Grace Hopper: Amazing Grace 14

Napoleon Bonaparte: Conqueror of Europe 16

Saladin: Warrior King 18

Joan of Arc: The Maid of Orléans 20

Horatio Nelson: The Greatest British Admiral 22

Michelle Howard: First Female Admiral in the US Navy 24

Sun Tzu: Warrior and Philosopher 26

More Military Leaders Who Changed the World 28

Glossary 30

Read More 31

Index 32

About the Author 32

1

Julius Caesar: The Man Who Made an Empire

A Gallic chiefton surrendors to Caesar after the Battle of Alesia in 52 BCE.

Julius Caesar was an important person in ancient Rome. He was born around 100 BCE. His family was in Rome's ruling class. He grew up to be a politician and a general. His army was well trained and tough. Caesar did whatever it took to win. His biggest success was adding to Rome's land.

Between 59 and 50 BCE, Caesar and his army fought a war in Gaul. Today, this area is France and parts of Belgium, Germany, and Italy. Caesar won battle after battle. He invaded Britain to fight people called the Celts. He was afraid the Celts would help Gaul. In the end, Gaul became part of Rome.

After Caesar conquered Gaul, he tried to go home to Rome. At the

75 BCE

Year when Caesar was captured by pirates

- Caesar was sailing to Rhodes to study public speaking.
- A band of pirates captured him and held him for 38 days.
- After Caesar was freed, he tracked down the pirates and captured them.

time, Rome was a republic ruled by senators. Caesar was popular with the people. However, the senators were afraid of him. They feared his power. They told him to give up his army. Instead, Caesar marched his army into Rome. A civil war broke out between Caesar and his enemies.

For several years, Caesar's army fought other Roman armies. Caesar's armies won in the end. He then made himself dictator for life. The Roman Republic was now the Roman Empire. Senators no longer led the people. Caesar ruled on his own.

The Tusculum bust is considered the only surviving sculpture of Caesar made during his lifetime, and dates from 50–40 BCE.

2

Khatol Mohammadzai: Jumping into the History Books

General Khatol Mohammadzai in 2012.

Khatol Mohammadzai is the first female general in Afghanistan. She was born in Kabul in 1966. At that time, men and women in Afghanistan had equal rights. Everyone had access to schools and good jobs. As a kid, she was able to go to school. She also played sports and loved airplanes.

The Soviet Union invaded her country in 1979. The Soviet war against Afghan forces lasted nine years. During the war, Mohammadzai joined the Afghan National Army. Army members came to her high school looking for recruits. She was only 17 when she joined the army. She became a paratrooper after training. Paratroopers jump from planes in battle.

Mohammadzai served in the army for six years during the Soviet War. She stayed in the army until 1996. Then the Taliban captured Kabul. They ordered all women to stay indoors at home. Mohammadzai could not serve in the army for six years.

THINK ABOUT IT

Mohammadzai was forced out of the army by the Taliban. That government did not view women as equal to men. Was it fair that she was forced out because she was a woman?

When the Taliban lost power, she went back to active duty.

During her career, Mohammadzai jumped more than 600 times. She is a leader and hero in Afghanistan. She was the first woman to train as a paratrooper. She was the first woman to earn the rank of general. Today, she is still in the army. It is her job to train new soldiers.

35

Number of male paratroopers Khatol Mohammadzai beat in a parachute competition

- Afghanistan held an international competition in 2004.
- The competition celebrated Afghan Independence Day.
- Mohammadzai was the only female in the competition. She won.

3 Ulysses S. Grant: The Man Who Saved the Union

Ulysses S. Grant was born in Ohio in 1822. He spent most of his life as a soldier. When he was young, his father sent him to West Point. He finished 21st of 39 students in his class. His record in school was not very good. However, he fought well for the US Army in his first war. Grant was a captain in the Mexican-American War (1846–1848). After the war, he was assigned to different places. He served the US Army in New York, Michigan, California, and Oregon.

Grant did not enjoy military service at first. He quit the army in 1854. For seven

General Ulysses Grant circa 1855–1865.

1863

Year when Union forces captured Vicksburg, Mississippi

- Ulysses S. Grant's victory at Vicksburg was a turning point in the Civil War.
- Earlier efforts to take the city had failed.
- Grant came up with a plan that proved his military genius.

Grant's victory at Vicksburg gave control of the Mississippi River to the Union.

years, he worked odd jobs. His first job was as a farmer in St. Louis, Missouri. He worked on his father-in-law's farm for six years. Then he worked as a clerk in a general store. He was living in Illinois when the Civil War started. Grant decided to join the army again.

He first led a volunteer group from Illinois. During the war, he rose in rank. He started as a colonel in 1861. When the war ended, he was General-in-Chief of the Union armies. Grant led an army with more soldiers than his enemy. He defeated several armies of the Confederacy. As the top general, his army moved across the South. His forces took one city at a time. He moved from Vicksburg, Mississippi, to Savannah, Georgia.

Grant showed no emotion. He was determined to win. As he moved east, he met Robert E. Lee's army. Grant and Lee were the top generals on each side. When Lee lost, the Civil War ended. Grant has been called the savior of the Union. He would later become the 18th president of the United States.

4 Queen Boudicca: From Teen to Warrior Queen

Boudicca was born in Britain in the year 30. In Celtic, her name means "victory." She was born in Colchester, England. Later in life, she would make history there.

A 1793 engraving of Queen Boudicca.

Boudicca married a king in the year 48. Prasutagus was that man. He was king of the Iceni tribe. Boudicca and Prasutagus had two daughters.

All Iceni women were trained to fight. Many became tough fighters. At the time, Rome ruled most of England. The Roman Empire had fought many tribes to win control. The Iceni had a truce with Rome. But when Boudicca's husband died in the year 60, Rome broke the truce.

Boudicca and her family suffered greatly. Her daughters were mistreated. Her land was taken. She fought back and united several Celtic tribes. She gathered an army of 100,000. Rome had the best army in the ancient world. But Boudicca would prove they were not perfect. She led her army to Colchester first. They beat the Roman defenders and destroyed the entire town. Later, Boudicca and her army beat Roman forces in London and St. Albans.

A statue of Boudicca and her daughter stands near Westminster Bridge in London.

Boudicca's goal was to kick the Roman Empire out of England. But Rome sent an elite army to face her. Boudicca's army was defeated. She died soon after. Her army did not have experience. Their weapons were poor. Boudicca did not achieve her goal. But she did show the world that Rome could be beaten.

BOUDICCA'S STORY LIVES ON

Tacitus, a Roman senator and historian, lived in the same time as Boudicca. He wrote down her story. Centuries later, copies were found in monastery libraries. Many people learned about Boudicca's bravery and strength. England's Queen Elizabeth I was inspired by Boudicca's example. So was Queen Victoria.

80,000

Estimated number of Roman soldiers killed by Boudicca's army

- Boudicca destroyed three of Rome's most important cities in England.
- Colchester was the Roman capital at this time.
- London is England's capital today, but back then it was small and undefended.

5

Charles Martel: The Man They Called "The Hammer"

Charles Martel was born in Francia in 688. His father, Pepin of Herstal, had more power than a king. At the time, Europe was not stable. Francia was split in two parts. One man ruled the west, and another ruled the east.

After his father died, Martel fought to reunite Francia. That war lasted from 715 to 718. Martel lost his first battle. But that was the only battle he ever lost. Martel used new tactics. He would attack at midday, while the enemy rested. Sometimes he would pretend to retreat. This lured his enemies into a trap. After three years, Martel beat the western kingdom. He now ruled all the Franks.

Martel fought more battles to protect his kingdom. He defeated forces from Holland in the north. He stopped Saxon armies in southern Germany. His greatest fight came against Islamic armies from Africa. The Moors conquered Spain in 711. From 711 to 730, they raided Francia. In 732, the Moors defeated Frankish forces in Bordeaux, France. Martel

Charles Martel at the Battle of Tours in 732.

5

Number of years Charles Martel fought Islamic armies

- The defeat of the Moors at Tours did not stop the Islamic advances.
- The son of the defeated Moorish leader invaded Francia in 736. Martel defeated him, too.
- Martel reclaimed important Frankish cities from Islamic rule by the end of 737.

GRANDFATHER TO A GREAT KING

Martel is credited with unifying Francia. He is also credited with saving Europe. His grandson, Charlemagne, was also a great leader. In his day, Charlemagne united most of Western Europe. Some call Charlemagne the father of Europe.

marched his armies to Tours that same year. At the Battle of Tours, his army defeated the Moors. The enemy leader was killed.

Charles won using new tactics. He used heavy cavalry and elite infantry in battle. He was truly "the Hammer" of his day.

Six ancestors of Charlemagne surround the base of his statue in Belgium, including Charles Martel.

Grace Hopper: Amazing Grace

Rear Admiral Grace Hopper.

Grace Hopper was born on December 9, 1906, in New York City. Her father was a graduate of Yale. Hopper grew up at a time when women didn't study math and science. She graduated from Vassar College in 1928 with degrees in math and physics. Then she went to Yale, her father's university. She earned her master's degree and her PhD, both in math. She taught math at Vassar.

Hopper joined the US Navy during World War II. She was assigned to a research project at Harvard. She learned to program a Mark I computer. After the war, she went to work for private companies that made computers. In 1952, she and her team created the first compiler. This is a program that turns English language instructions into code computers can understand. Her work led to the computer language known as COBOL. That stands for Common Business-Oriented Language. By the 1970s, COBOL was the most-used computer language in the world.

Hopper retired from the Naval Reserve in 1966. But she was soon called back to active duty. The Navy wanted her to work on their computer languages and programs. When Hopper retired again in 1986, she was 79 years old. She was the oldest serving officer in the US armed forces. She was also a rear admiral. When Hopper died in 1992, she was buried in Arlington National cemetery with full military honors.

Hopper in her computer room in 1978..

40+

Honorary degrees awarded to Grace Hopper

- In 1991, Hopper received the National Medal of Technology.
- In 1996, the US Navy named a destroyer the *USS Hopper.*
- In 2016, Hopper posthumously received the Presidential Medal of Freedom.

GRACE HOPPER COINED THE TERM "BUG"

While working at Harvard, Hopper came up with a term used a lot today. A computer she was working on had an unknown problem. It turns out a moth got into the circuits. Today, people use the term "bug" to describe unknown problems.

7 Napoleon Bonaparte: Conqueror of Europe

Napoleon Bonaparte was born on August 15, 1769, on the island of Corsica. His father was from a noble Italian family. Napoleon went to school in France. He graduated from an elite French military academy. At 16, he became a commissioned officer.

In 1793, Napoleon led the French to victory at Toulon, a city in southern France. After that, he was promoted

Napoleon Bonaparte in 1812.

2,800

Number of British soldiers who guarded Napoleon on St. Helena

- Europe did not want Napoleon to return to power ever again.
- The soldiers were there to make sure he did not escape.
- The force included 500 cannons and 11 ships.

One of Napoleon's great victories was at the Battle of Marengo in Italy in 1800.

to brigadier general. In 1796, he took over the French army in Italy. He won important battles there. When he returned to Paris, he was a hero. In 1799, he overthrew the French government. He put himself in charge. Within a few years, he named himself Emperor. Napoleon was the first Emperor of France.

The years from 1799 to 1815 are called the Napoleonic Era. Napoleon's armies fought with almost every country in Europe. By 1811, France controlled most of Europe. But then Napoleon made a big mistake. In 1812, he invaded Russia with a huge army. As Napoleon's army advanced, the Russian army pulled back. But first, they destroyed everything around them. Napoleon's army had no food or shelter. Hundreds of thousands of French troops died. Napoleon suffered another defeat in 1813, this time in Germany.

Back in France, Napoleon gave up being emperor. He was exiled to the island of Elba. He escaped, gathered an army, and marched on Paris. He went back to being emperor. But that did not last long. When the French lost the Battle of Waterloo, Napoleon was exiled to the island of St. Helena. He died there in 1821.

THINK ABOUT IT

Another nation tried to invade Russia in 1941. Find out what happened.

8

Saladin: Warrior King

Saladin was born in Tikrit, Iraq, in 1137. His birth name was Yusuf ibn Ayyub. He became Saladin later in life. He was a Muslim military leader and politician. His uncle Asad al-Dīn Shīrkūh taught him the art of war. He also taught Saladin philosophy and law.

In 1169, Shīrkūh and Saladin led an army to Egypt. They forced a Christian army to leave the city of Cairo. This was during the Crusades. The Crusades were a series of religious wars between Christians and Muslims. The Christian armies were called Crusaders. Shīrkūh took control of Cairo. After Shīrkūh died, Saladin became the ruler of the city.

Saladin circa 1552–1568.

Then the leader of the Muslim empire died. Saladin proclaimed himself sultan of all Egypt. He conquered Syria, Palestine, and Yemen. He took cities away from rival Muslim leaders. He unified the empire. After his victories, he became known as Saladin. The name means "Righteousness of the Faith."

The Crusaders had held Jerusalem since 1099. Saladin wanted it back. But first, he had to beat an army of Crusaders. He did this by setting a trap. He attacked a smaller city to draw them out. Then, when the Crusaders marched into

Syrian Crusaders surrendering to Saladin.

the hot, dry desert, he attacked them. He defeated them at the Battle of Hattin in 1187. After that, Jerusalem surrendered.

1095–1291

Years when the Crusades were fought

- By the end of the eleventh century, Muslims ruled much of the ancient Christian world.
- Both Christians and Muslims wanted to control sites they considered sacred.
- One of the most sacred sites was the city of Jerusalem.

SUNNIS AND SHIITES

A sect is a group within a religious faith. Two sects may have very different beliefs. Sunni and Shiite are two sects in the Islamic faith. They have had big disagreements since the year 634. These have led to conflicts and violence. Saladin was a Sunni Muslim. Shiites tried to assassinate him twice.

9

Joan of Arc: The Maid of Orléans

Joan of Arc was born in France in 1412. She called herself Joan the Maid. History remembers her as the Maid of Orléans. That name comes from her great victory at the city of Orléans.

During Joan's life, France and England were fighting the Hundred Years War. Both countries wanted control of France. At the age of 14, Joan started hearing voices and having visions. She believed that God was calling her to fight for France. When she was 17, Joan went to meet France's Prince Charles. He had a chance to claim the throne. But he needed someone to fight for him.

Charles did not believe that Joan was having visions from God. At first, he tried to trick her. He dressed in common clothes and acted like everyone else in the room. But Joan knew him right away. She bowed before the rightful King of France. He gave her an army. Still only 17, Joan led the army to Orléans. The city was under siege by the English. She attacked them. Struck by an arrow, she kept fighting. Her forces won.

Joan of Arc as depicted on a 1504 parchment manuscript.

SAINT JOAN

Joan was put to death for going against the Catholic Church. Five hundred years later, the Catholic Church made her a saint. She is also the patron saint of France.

70

Number of charges Joan faced during her trial

- Joan was tried as a heretic.
- She was charged with not obeying the commands of the Church.
- She was also charged with witchcraft and dressing like a man.

When Charles VII was crowned King of France, Joan was there. A year later, she fought another battle against the English. This time, she was captured and imprisoned. Later, she was tried and put to death. She was only 19. Today, Joan is remembered as a brave warrior.

Joan of Arc at the coronation of Charles VII.

10

Horatio Nelson: The Greatest British Admiral

A portrait of Admiral Horatio Nelson from 1898 that includes the chelengk he wore on his hat.

WHAT'S THAT ON HIS HAT?

Many portraits of Nelson show him wearing a big hat. On the hat is a fancy decoration called a chelengk. It is set with more than 300 diamonds. It was given to Nelson by the Sultan of Turkey after the Battle of the Nile.

Horatio Nelson was born in Norfolk, England, in 1758. He was the sixth of 11 children. His parents were poor. Nelson would become a great naval commander. He is remembered for winning important battles.

Nelson joined the Royal Navy at age 12. His first naval battle was against an animal. At 14, he was on a mission to the Arctic Circle. He defended a small boat against a walrus.

Nelson served the Royal Navy around the world. He served in the West Indies during the American Revolution. He served in the Mediterranean during the French Revolution. Nelson was promoted to lieutenant. Then he was made a captain and given his own ship.

Nelson fought France and Spain during the Napoleonic Wars. Led by Napoleon, this was a series of wars against most of the rest of Europe. In 1798, Nelson beat a French fleet in the Battle of the Nile. Napoleon had planned to invade Egypt. Nelson stopped him.

3 Horatio Nelson's injuries

- In 1794, during the siege of Calvi, Nelson lost most of the sight in his right eye.
- In 1797, during the Battle of Santa Cruz de Tenerife, he was shot in his right arm. It was amputated.
- His gunshot wound at Trafalgar in 1805 was fatal.

Officers rescue Nelson after he was wounded at the Battle of Santa Cruz de Tenerife.

Nelson came up with unique tactics. He would also ignore rules if he thought he could win. His greatest victory was at the Battle of Trafalgar in 1805. Napoleon wanted to invade England. Nelson's Royal Navy fleet defeated Napoleon's fleet. England was saved. But Nelson had been shot by a sniper. His funeral was held at St. Paul's Cathedral. A nation mourned.

11

Michelle Howard: First Female Admiral in the US Navy

Michelle Howard was born in California in 1960. She came from a military family. Her dad was in the US Air Force. When Howard was 12, she decided to join the military when she grew up. At the time, few women were accepted into the military. Even fewer were given powerful spots. Howard would change that.

Women could not go to military academies until 1976. In high school, Michelle applied to the US Naval Academy. She was accepted in 1978. Her class had 1,363 students. Michelle was one of seven African-American women in the class. She graduated in 1982. Then she went to the Army's Command and General Staff College. She graduated in 1998 with a master's degree. Her degree was in military arts and sciences.

Admiral Michelle Howard.

Michelle Howard broke barriers. She served many sea tours aboard several ships. She rose through the ranks. She was a chief engineer and a first lieutenant. Then she was an executive officer. In 1999, she took command of her own ship, the USS *Rushmore*. Howard was the

Howard meeting with US sailors in 2009.

35

Years Michelle Howard served in the US Navy

- She trained on cruisers, submarines, and even an aircraft carrier.
- She deployed around the world to places like the Pacific Ocean, Atlantic Ocean, Mediterranean Sea, and Adriatic Sea.
- She also held many jobs onshore in the Navy. For example, she was the 38th Vice Chief of Naval Operations.

first African-American woman to command a US Navy ship.

In 2009, she took command of Expeditionary Strike Group Two. She was the first African-American woman to lead a US Navy battle group. It guarded the Persian Gulf and worked in the Indian Ocean. Sailors under Howard's command rescued Captain Richard Phillips from Somali pirates. In 2014, Howard was promoted to four-star admiral. She was the first woman to reach this rank. Howard retired from the US Navy in 2017.

12

Sun Tzu: Warrior and Philosopher

Sun Tzu was born in China in 544 BCE. Little is known about his childhood. His family was from the upper class of society. Sun Tzu showed an interest in warfare early in life. He also learned to write well. He is believed to have written a book called *The Art of War*.

Sun Tzu was a military strategist and general. He served the King of Wu. He showed great skill at leading soldiers. He also knew many tactics to use in battle. Even though he was skilled in battle, he did not

Portrait of Sun Tzu from the China Military Museum in Beijing.

13

Number of chapters in Sun Tzu's *The Art of War*

- Sun Tzu wrote, "Who wishes to fight must first count the cost."
- Sun Tzu wrote, "The supreme art of war is to subdue the enemy without fighting."
- Sun Tzu wrote, "The greatest victory is that which requires no battle."

A MILITARY LEADER WHO AVOIDED WAR

Sun Tzu wrote the most famous book on military strategy. But he believed war should be avoided. If people had to fight, it was important to win as quickly as possible. Long wars harmed the winner, too.

Sun Tzu's book *The Art of War* on bamboo, a traditional Chinese book making material, from the Qing dynasty (1735–1796).

always fight. Sun Tzu believed in fighting only when he knew he could win.

The Art of War includes Sun Tzu's ideas on military strategy. One of his best tips was about flexibility. To win, armies needed a flexible strategy. If the battle changed, the strategy needed to change.

Sun Tzu displayed his skills and tactics while serving the King of Wu. That kingdom went to war against the Chu state. Chu had more soldiers. Their soldiers had better skills. But Sun Tzu had disciplined troops. He also had better strategies. With soldiers who listened and obeyed, Sun Tzu won the battle. He would win several more battles. In the end, Sun Tzu took Chu's capital city of Ying.

His military victories made him successful. His book made him legendary. Generals still read his book today. So do business leaders. Almost anyone can learn something from Sun Tzu's book.

More Military Leaders Who Changed the World

Charlemagne

Charlemagne's name means "Charles the Great." He was born around 747 and died around 814. He was King of the Franks and grandson of Charles Martel. He united most of Europe for the first time since the Roman Empire. Under Charlemagne's rule, France expanded greatly. Charlemagne fought the Moors in Spain and spread Christianity across Europe.

Queen Elizabeth I

Elizabeth I was Queen of England for 45 years. She was born in 1533 and died in 1603. Her rule is known as a golden age in English history. England became a major European power. The kingdom showed off its political, economic, and military might. Elizabeth's biggest achievement was her defense against a Spanish invasion. Under her leadership, the Royal Navy beat the Spanish Armada.

Elizabeth's hand rests on a globe to symbolize her international power after defeating the Spanish Armada.

Robert E. Lee

Robert E. Lee led the Confederate Army during the US Civil War. He was born in 1807 and died in 1870. His father was a hero in the American Revolutionary War. Lee graduated from the US Army academy at West Point. He first served in the US Army. He fought in the Mexican-American War. Lee won many battles during the Civil War, even though his army often had fewer soldiers and supplies.

Mustafa Kemal Ataturk

Mustafa Kemal Ataturk was born in 1881 in the Ottoman Empire and died in 1938 in Istanbul. Ataturk fought against the ruling sultans in the empire. He led Turkish forces in the Turkish War of Independence. He founded the Republic of Turkey and helped to modernize the country. He also set laws that kept religion and the state separate.

Mustafa Kemal Ataturk circa 1930.

Glossary

barrier
Something, physical or not, that blocks a path to a goal or destination.

elite
The best of a class; people who exercise a lot of power or influence.

heretic
Someone whose beliefs go against official beliefs.

kingdom
A community or nation with a king or queen in control.

philosophy
A type of education that looks for wisdom in all things.

pioneer
A person or group among the first to achieve a goal.

posthumous
Happening after someone's death.

republic
A form of government with a leader that is not a queen or king.

rightful
An act or position that is deserved or earned.

tactics
The art or skill of moving forces in combat.

Taliban
An Islamic militant group in Afghanistan.

territory
A place under the control of an outside government.

voyage
The act of traveling long distances, generally at sea.

Read More

Donovan, Sandy. *Lethal Leaders and Military Madmen.* Shock Zone: Villains. Minneapolis, MN: Lerner Publications, 2013.

Gigliotti, Jim. *Who Was Napoleon?* Who Was...?. New York: Penguin Workshop, 2018.

Waterfield, Kathryn, and Robin Waterfield. *Who Was Alexander the Great?* Who Was...?. New York: Penguin Workshop, 2016.

Index

Ataturk, Mustafa Kemal, 29
avoided war, 26-27

Battle of Trafalgar, 23
Battle of Waterloo, 17
Bonaparte, Napoleon, 16-17, 23, 31

Caesar, Julius, 4-5
Charlemagne, 13, 28
Civil War, 8-9, 29
computer languages, 14
Crusaders, 18-19

Emperor of France, 17

first woman:
- to train as paratrooper, 7
- rank of general, 7
- rank of four-star admiral, 25

Grant, Ulysses S., 8-9

Hopper, Grace, 14-15
Howard, Michelle, 24-25

Joan of Arc, 20-21

Lee, Robert E., 9, 29

Martel, Charles, 12-13, 28
Mohammadzai, Khatol, 6-7

Nelson, Horatio, 22-23

Queen Boudicca, 10-11
Queen Elizabeth I, 11, 28
Roman Empire, 5, 10-11, 28
Royal Navy, 22-23, 28

Saladin, 18-19
Sun Tzu, 26-27

tactics, 12, 23, 26-27, 30
Taliban, 6-7, 30
The Art of War, 26-27

unification:
- Francia, 13
- Western Europe, 13
- Muslim Empire, 18

Union Armies, 8-9
US Navy, 14-15, 24-25

women warriors, 10-11, 20-21

About the Author

Matthew McCabe is an experienced freelance writer. He's previously written other children's books for 12-Story Library including *12 Business Leaders Who Changed the World* and *12 Political Leaders Who Changed the World*. He lives in Plymouth, Minnesota, with his wife, daughter, and son.